John Seed

Also by John Seed:

Spaces In (Pig Press, Newcastle-upon-Tyne 1977)

History Labour Night. Fire & Sleet & Candlelight (Pig Press, Durham 1984)

Transit Depots (Ship of Fools, London 1993)

Interior in the Open Air (Reality Street, London 1993)

Divided into One (Poetical Histories, Cambridge 2003)

Pictures from Mayhew. London 1850 (Shearsman Books, Exeter 2005)

New and Collected Poems

John Seed

Shearsman Books
Exeter

First published in in the United Kingdom in 2005 by
Shearsman Books Ltd
58 Velwell Road
Exeter EX4 4LD

www.shearsman.com

ISBN 0-907562-63-9

Cover based on a design by poppodomedia.com
Cover photograph by John Seed.

Acknowledgements
Thanks are due to those who first published the books collected in this
volume: Richard and Ann Caddel (Pig Press), Robert Sheppard and
Patricia Farrell (Ship of Fools), Ken Edwards (Reality Street Editions)
and Peter Riley (Poetical Histories).

Some of the uncollected poems published here previously appeared in
CCCP Review, Chicago Review, Cultural Logic and *Great Works*.

The publisher gratefully acknowledges financial assistance from Arts Council
England.

CONTENTS

Spaces In (1977)

History Labour Night (1984)   29

SPACES IN

1977

THE QUEEN   If trembling of my limbs or sudden tears
Proclaim your song beyond denial best,
I leave these corridors, this ancient house,
A famous throne, the reverence of servants –
What do I gain?

SWINEHERD   A song – the night of love,
An ignorant forest and the dung of swine.

W.B.Yeats, *A Full Moon in March*

a little wind disturbs the curtain

The unmarked page

is never blank

Lindisfarne : Dole

England's coast a shadow
Over the grey water. Morning
Rain dripping from everything.
Far from the village,
Faces stone, stung by wind, we
Trudge the shore. Kelp
Knee-deep, a cormorant
Low over the bay below the
Castle. In silence
Walking, dreamless for hours.
Everything
We need but forced
To leave as if we wanted to

                    headlights of the great lorries
                              flashing
        speed and movement "a kind of redemption"
                    surging rhythm of the
                              engine in the empty
streets
              a metaphysic   direction of events
                    second by second
        shines on passing windscreens   wing-mirrors
              outward

a hundred yards

to the South the Humber to the East

moves

or the carriage

each second the height of a man

image ?

distance   distance

desolate riverside warehouse

no image no

language

beyond the glass   the specific the vast

winter sun silver over the waves

the sweep of the estuary

in the morning light the streets
quiet

      and further downstream
the glitter of metal and glass
through the bright haze

cranes silent along the dockside

the wind   moving among leaves moving
among shadow of leaves
        between trees   the invisible text
                second by second changing
                     and change in this
air of backrooms   kitchens
        paint flaking from the lintel
            other layers other
            colours   decades the mad
whirlpool of event
            continues
                second by second
things are lost   left behind
minute by minute earth fades underfoot   names
blurred on old gravestones
        shadows dancing on bright grass in
sunlight the flame invisible a dream   the world
                     another
place the arbitrary the intended
            myth the circular
        horizon of multiple thresholds
        windswept hills
a fragile sapling
        stem snapped by a recent gust
low hills over which clouds drift......

Never to forget......
     the dreamlessness of time   never
to forget for an instant
the instruments of torture the gleaming
precisions

              in the soft earth the tip
of a spear
hurled
through Millenia of
Space

Stalactite & Stalagmite

one millimetre in ten years . . .
a process of addition
human and not human the
shining ancient rock
stalagmite   "Mother and Child"
human shape of stone
as if earth intended
images our lives we walk between

After Time

in the night the night
wind   voices
echo
        in the small street
                            shadows
moving   carried along I think

"...the absolute projection of an object
of the origin of which no account can
be given with the result that the space
between projection and thing projected
is dark and void . . . "

unknown
        the
unknown
        footsteps fade

Not speaking we
Stare out   linked
To a matrix a kind of
Language
Each instant the point
Where we are
Shared   if it is possible
Keeps the mind
Off blank walls the open door
In twilight the path winding
Back   the way we came

Minds would leave each
other in contrary directions,
traverse each other in
Numberless points, and at
last greet each other
at the Journey's end — "

Tired,
and so strangely distant,
so tired of strange places

These hours
The tides

in the fierce wind in the
moonlight

these frozen spaces
stretch
       North
     'owing tribute to no
     Southern king
          before Athelstan'

still the cold flame
sparkling on the dark water the boundaries
extending

                    out of the north on the
Spring winds
Terror

          a taut sail on the horizon
          or where the sea
          wars against the river
        sixteen pairs of oars of pine
Striking the water in unison:

Generations feared

Over Oceanus Germanicus

Easterly
          the Spring winds

Immensities of stone the centuries
Small sounds of birds in the guttering

A web of occurrence

                    in medias res the mind
Connects
                coincidence a paradigm
                the beautiful face of Isabella
                daughter and sister of France
                wife of England   a label-stop
                on the wall of the south aisle of the nave
                carved in the time of Chaucer
                Athelstan   staring into blackness
                white limestone cool to the touch

                'Were beth they biforen us weren ?'

Where they were   here and not here

Where we stand together on
Cold stone   'In-Derawuda'

Into What Depth Thou Seest
From What Height Fallen

Walking   in darkness

Between the trees

As already we'd
Dreamed   a stone path
Curves along the shore   We
Step over the thick roots

In the shadow of leaves
Watch the nightworld

What offered no alternative   up
Turned   brilliant on the dark water all
The distances of sky the
Nothingness at the centre

Here at our feet

Opposite within opposite the

Spaces in the heart

Backstreet

Sun brightening up on the brick
Opposite   over the piled books
These spaces the mind moves through eyes
Like beams of light in abstracto
The pattern of streets our friends the
Sparrows flickering around the yards
Filch bread and baconscraps
In the alley ivy and willowherb growing
In the muck
        in the quiet air

History Labour Night
Fire & Sleet & Candlelight

1984

Represented in the inmost cell of thought is
that which is unlike thought

T.W. Adorno *Negative Dialectics*

The dream   if

It was a dream…it was

Not a dream

Lines in Wasdale Head

horizontal on rough grass

For an hour or more

Sleepless I dreamt you here across the spaces the

Silent presence of another discourse

Impenetrable as the limitless

Sky the sky's lights in meaningless pattern the

Whole structure swivels on an axis

Inserted in the earth somewhere

In these dark fields   nightwind whispers of

It whispers of you

Nightshift

Far out in the estuary all night
A boat's foghorn   hour
After hour   like a stone in a
Stream at the centre of consciousness

       . . . dark water the haze

Impenetrable   England's coast this
Alien place

Ragged clouds in the wind
Over Holland before dawn

Saltwater foaming on shingle along Spurn

Alien powers

In the mind but in space I

Stand at the window   image
Thrown back on glass against blackness

Far out in the estuary all night
The boat's foghorn   intelligible sphere

External to everything

'This Curious Involvement,
A Dominant Species'

In memory of John Riley

Smoke twisting over the scorched ground
In the shadow of sky little disc
Ablaze

through the fields and the hills
Last leaves like snow
blown through space

Everything converged to this

silence

endless play of reflection

Actual tree-root twisting through dry earth

Absolute presence   dazzling, impenetrable

Always there always different in
Human matrix

Little world these quiet woodlands

In a tangle of connections

Happy unhappy coincidence
Eye of the storm

December 1978

After Walter Benjamin

Storm blowing from the beginning

History history's angel
Hurled backwards into future
        tattered wings spread, ears deafened
Watches the debris climb skyward

                                        shattered
Crystal of human reason

There *was* no beginning

A room without doors
Through which the wind blows always we

Shelter in language

Tiny souls patched up for heaven

meanings change

Hundreds and thousands of days
Unrecoverable past an inflexion of tone November
Light flickering in the gale

Shape of cloud above the wildness childhood sepia stories
We tell ourselves   made of shadows

Meanings shift and dissolve

Hard world the mute accomplice
Sleeps without dream

Diamond heart

open sea the open sky

Drenched spaces and whispering
   Forms of existence now as
Always a multiple exposure on the
   German ocean the morning light   out
      Past Spurn Head difficult
   To imagine a southern shore here the
Edge of a forest curved
   Now shining water white sky
     From here to Jutland

The centre is space now
                    in the dusk slowly
          circles in the broken water
watching the great tankers float by the
          great wheel of circulation
                                        unkind
from such knowledge go from the door
          sleep in the outer room the blue fabrics
                    like milk in the yard the moon
                              comes to the gate
                    bright with Jupiter overhead
(alcohol he went upstairs

During War, The Timeless Air

the sea shone
and we walked in danger
To the cliff-edge

Soft grass   immensity of cloudless
Space

gulls guillemots   a dark bird
Whose name we never knew

Everywhere
their sound among the white rocks . . .

But we are dumb

Powerless   now totally exposed . . .

Shivering naked into space the

Solitary mind flickers among elements

In silence

For a moment almost free

At the nation's edge
Bede's image of
Was it?   a sparrow
Swooping through the bright hall

England May 1982

'History teaches, but it has no pupils'

Gramsci

I

we inherited dreams

Woke up in a strange place alone among shadows
Rain blowing in from the North Sea in
Soft blue twilight the lamps come on

Relation   absence of relation
Imagining the real   unimagined contradictions

. . . to make poetry of these streets
Hours and days
contemplating a page a line a word

pale children in broken shoes
unteachable and silent
in the mad tangle of languages

Shimmer of streetlamps on the glazed roads
Rain falling through darkness

. . . a place different from this

II

Locked within a human matrix the
Park is quiet
        ducks drift dreaming on the murky pool
Then converge towards us
             we have no bread no message

Rooted in history   the nightshift begins again

Perfect sky first star   in a tangle of branches
Incoherent
        tangle of
             moments

      . . . street after street and between   the
Masts of the trawlers

  shed for the waiting taxis
    chalk on the crumbling brick

Beneath amber lamps through confusion
Who could I have been who
Could have changed this . . .

                  irrelevant

       as irrelevant as meaning perhaps

From Ric Caddel's Back Kitchen Window

Mile after mile the wet roads the weak light
Empty streets
In plenitude of nature
Windswept
In freezing rain in silence that
Familiar place
Dark hills huge clouds blank
Stone on these slopes the same
End from any source

A thousand stratagems

Vanishing into the air

                      ego

Scriptor

From Manchester
To George and Mary Oppen in San Francisco

                    this city has its beggars too
Lonely and threadbare in bronchial gloom
                    like the sparrows
Imagining bread or Spring
                                    . . . or the solitary
Traveller   here and not here
In the crowded night of streets
Dreaming each footstep
Home

            indecipherable

            ache beneath the ribs

In the Sweet Dark

                    between statements I
Walk among the trees
Along a dark lane   alone no longer
Relating discourse to experience?
Tracks   criss-crossing
Bare black wet branches
Fracturing into the chill air like breath . . .

Returning , again and again

What was it I left behind last night?
On the train rattling through the black fields
Till I woke before dawn

                    . . . mist over the fields the worn footpath
A dog barking
                    stupidly insistent

in the morning isolate we
Huddle in private bodies along the platform imaginary
Subjects   ghosts
Of the structure of the
Language of the circuit of capital . . .
Imaginary keys to a real door locked iron
Rails the bitter wind a mouthful of broken glass

To Wait by the River

in the noon heat

In the shadow of the bridge the

Flickering light on the water

Sticklebacks flickering
In the warm shallow water evading
Capture   one English summer
Circa 1959 . . .

Bright window of bare sky
Over the river the same

Child's face bent

Over the water   invisible
Boundaries   unravelling

Through his fingers my fingers the baffling

Stream

Petuaria

Deep irregular chime of the new
Marker off Brough Roads

Adrift out there in the night the mist the cold

Consciousness   a ghost . . .

Intervals silently drifting

Vapour obscures the stars the starlit

Humber's glittering

Tide in imagination Romans waded
Muddied waters in the wake of
Conquest

Wherever we're headed

Hushed midstream the water's edge

INTERIOR IN THE OPEN AIR

1993

'even in the most sublimated work of art
there is a hidden "it should be different"...'
Theodor Adorno

Cloud formations shift in the evening air
Clear almost to infinity over the
Crowded rooftops

Stars starlight brilliant   random

                as the pattern of streets in
Achromatic light
Actual pavements almost invisible 'I wake

From daydreams to this

Real night'

            . . . meaning is difficult
                                detours
Across darkness

Between language and silence struggling

For breath seeking roots in stone the shabby
Corridors of the underground echoing

Footsteps   a distant shout

ALONG THE THAMES, LOOKING FROM THE ROOF OF THE CUSTOM HOUSE: October 1849

Light filtered through the tangled rigging and the masts – sails looped in festoons to the yards.

Barges filled with barrels of beer, sacks of flour. Hoys, deep in the moving water, tarpaulins covering the heaped-up cargoes. A schooner and a brig, both from Spain, laden with fruit. Black-looking colliers. Russian brigs from Memel and Petersburg. Lug boats. Empty lighters. Dutch eel boats of polished oak – round bluff bows and green-tipped rudders. Huge steamers with gilt sterns and mahogany wheels, bright brass binnacles glittering in the late sun. Sloops filled with cases of wine, bales of hemp, barrels of port, crates of hardware.

Busy trade and boundless capital: all corners of the earth ransacked, each for its peculiar produce.

A sort of trade.

Axis mundi.

BRICK LANE MARKET

Denturescrackedjugsbrokenshoespanlids. Collar studs for shirts long since rags.

Detritus. Wish-symbols of another generation. Bent figures in the afternoon sifting garbage in the gutters. Circulation of commodities at the limit.

Human figures bent over the gutters sifting garbage.

September 1984

Roofscape outlined black against the
changing sky as the streets grow blue with
dawn. Early workers gather round the
breakfast stall, blowing saucers of steaming
coffee. Little slattern girl, basket slung
before her, screams watercresses through
the sleeping avenues.

London, October 1849

Fifty thousand nights and
Chill dawns . . .   structures
Fade upward into grey
Morning into afternoon   history
In alien familiar streets
Gone haywire written
Before under the same blank
Sky all
Lifelines converge the crystal mists the track
Veers into obscurity peters out
Into bramble fern barbed wire

Alien territory

                              our minds are blank
Or less than blank . . .

                              in the drab light the
Embarkation for Cytherea

Image then black

Like a candle blown out

. . . image   images

Of capital in drifting smoke
          Brief shadows moving
Across darkness and the flickering
Light of blazing cars

Lost in tangles of discourse

     . . . another rainy night in Raynes Park
          among the surfaces of
               things blurred
                    a kind of path

Down into the crater's core

There is no form for this leaden structure.
Metropolitan grey, the great cold slabs of
power, all that excludes and does not change,
becoming more itself. It is the water moves,
beside the bare embankment, the chill dream . . .
Contingency. Or there is only form. Repetition
on repetition, impenetrable, the ungraspable
figure of what we should have known.

What had to be believed to be seen. More
absorbed within itself, fading into complexity it
ends abruptly, or continues outside all experience
its relentless trajectory. Or shifts for an instant
sideways, into the brightness that lifts from the
water the shining stones

Trudging the verb
Into streets   where else
SW19 SW20
Victorian property after
Dark surfaces all
Changed in five years

Indifference the local
Currency   meaningless
Succession of signs
Shopfronts stretch
Limos   merchants
Of space

What can be said here
Has to be imagined or

Imagine

Pale smudge the moon

or the female skeleton in a sweat
at the back of the Junction selling
meat to strangers

Different distances to convert
into the currency of meaning

Along the Rio Grande Russia
is going home

so couldn't you make this 'Art' too?
And so easy. The drab contingencies of a
Saturday afternoon, April 1988, in Stockwell.
As it happens. Almost in spirals the blown
dust, cigarette smoke, theories of M3 on
the bookies' doorsteps. Sharp, clear-edged,
against the shabby urban skyline the usual
world

                    beauty protected by almost, in its
cheap transcendence, its shoddy marketing
strategies

What used to be the sky again

Out of the azimuth west different
Clouds stream smoking colour Morden
Chaos small
Disturbances local detail
Slightest fluctuations

Changed everything

After
　　　　　of all places

The river glitters and seems to flow all ways. But the path is human, punctuated by orange pools that barely mirror a still sky. Half the morning I've walked here in my head whispering to you stories without narrative. Seeking clarity, daylight.

We left our happiness unwillingly.

It was more perfect than we knew

                out of the warm continuous rain
White willow catkins
Opening over the water
And all that is not
Here fugitive
Sounds   to make a synthesis to

Choose silence

MOONRISE, SNOW FLURRIES, NIGHTFALL: JANUARY 15TH,1987

                              staring beyond syntax icy
Configurations   leafless

Against the blackness

Inventing nothing

Mare Imbrium Mare Chrisium

Orion   tilting seaward

Over a street like any
Other it is possible

To imagine imagine to
Keep the dream

Approaching the dreamless the
Actual
Roots   reach down

        against the whiteness the mirror the
            smouldering ground

unrealities of human speech

                              what is it?
Unwrites these places   Words
Blown away like mist
Stirring the moist grass
Clings to thin soil in cracks
Between stones in an empty square the

Connectedness of things   dreaming itself . . .

There is no language now no letter
Will reach you   Tonight

I stood there again

In the silence in the moonlight empty

Hands your fingers tips clutching
The impossible surface

NIGHTSHIFT: GRAVES BAKERY, CHESTER-LE-STREET, AUGUST 1968

in memoriam Raymond Williams

                                        August then

Air looking into space I remember
The canteen empty before dawn huge
Windows night rain blurs
Almost vertically across the lorry park the
Patterns of light   and shadow
Sheltering smoking consolation 1968
Out of the foreman's sight

To wish it were otherwise

Nostalgia's bitter hope

Night rain corrodes

The little amber lamps threaded
Across low hills west the
Local resistances lonely
Category chosen

                                        January 1988

Sometimes it is always
Autumn already in the evening air
And the impossible brightness falls
And falls
Aching
Over the long hills west to
Cross Fell
                    estuaries of seacloud
Shadows
Up over the fell's rough bracken I imagine
Drifting out of time
Apart
From the child who was hurt where
I cannot go

in memoriam Louis Zukofsky

                              outside the dream no
Verb
Invented this freezing rain is this
The question riveted into brick
Under the bridge

Rust   edges

Already flaking

Slowly in October
Rain the transient structures the

So resistance shrinks to these

Shadow games the shallow

Strategies of noun verb noun

I meant to say something different

Child's eyes   impossible light

Believe for me

Singular waking
To the moment's strange
Radiance

   'that art carries its negation in itself
Like a telos'

Incomplete

Inside the gale

Brilliance   of moonlight

Shattered alternatives crossing
Water the clarities

Of form

Which is never enough

Aberdyfi 18 viii 1989

shadow of the gable-end
Sharp against the white wall
Fading and shifting
As clouds cross how beautiful
The world seems its transformations
Incomplete as we
Begin to leave

Silence inside the empty nouns
Though the paving stones
Through a corridor of trees
Details picturing
Voices at midnight single footsteps
Barely audible
A disturbance of the air moving
From one cause to the next
Through the city's anti-narrative the
A to Z
And stars   so many
Cloud after luminous cloud past
Shaping tomorrow drops quietly
Outside   without us
Whichever direction it's to

NEW YEAR'S EVE, 1989. DRIVING SOUTH

                    this is the year's last day
          and the decade's

One after another
Into the twilight the
Shifting circle of the visible

In the haze over Durham
The lines blur

Wherever we belonged

Toppling over the horizon
Behind us blueish
Whatever's the opposite
Of a construction site
Distributed North

What were we meant
To feel if not political
Hate?   and failure . . .

Poverty lies and despair

'We must suffer them all again'

And again

Little houses scattered
Lights of windows
Vulnerable under the dark

On the other side of language

Where do the dreaming kids
In the back seat come from speaking
Or not speaking
What kind of English
History can I tell them?

Migrants   intently we
Study the map for ideas
Though the single road
Revolves under the wheels
One direction three hundred miles

Where are we headed?
Not even exile
In such haste towards
Where we still face

The year's and the day's
The decade's
Deep midnight

'From Escomb, County Durham': July 1990

Reporting to a future difficult
To believe exists exactly
Midnight and actual rain
Out there beginning
Somewhere
Saxon car bodies rusting in
Empty yards nettles
Bramble wild roses hawthorn
Along the abandoned railway other
Names probably and blurred
Stonework the medium
Vertical of meaning
Lights the instant
Glitters if what you see
Circular in the organised
Silence diamond
Broaching and chancel arch
Serpent dial

Breathing in   the summer rushing
Past outside

'Best wishes'

CROSSING WESTMINSTER BRIDGE, NIGHTS, NOVEMBER 1990

1

    changing the words the
State's bevelled facets
Gleam on the water
Dark's throat whispering
Galleries

Where truth lies

Choking

An allegory of English
        and all night at the edge
Of hearing
        the police sirens

2

Torn into new forms

England's derelict
Archive 1990

An empty rectangle the
Empty house

To inherit

Where a picture was taken down

Weightless

Our shadows as we pass

3

Cold impenetrable
Steel plate the national index
Under the bridges below
Zero

Kerbstone houseroom homeland

Before dawn the morning tide

Sweet Thames
                    wherever you've come from
Fuck off

for Robert Sheppard & Patricia Farrell

                        but the precision

Of light   on asphalt crystal

For an instant

Outside

          the present

Tense   presence

         the future we

Disappear into

Quarter moon moving right

No-one

On the turn of Lessingham Avenue SW18

21.41

November 24th 1990

Passing each
Other in
Opposite directions

An old kind of unhappiness

For the witness
No-one bears witness . . .

In any language

Ist ein Land verloren

Sans souci: without cares

Buried here after two centuries
Where he intended again
Beside his dogs
Under the Prussian sky white
Distance the
Order of things

Particulars

Arranged accurately
The oblivion of fact

Potsdam, 30 March 1992

Empty chairs around
This single bed this table the
Absent   know their names
Wherever you're sleeping
The privatization of shared facilities
Ghosts of language
In me imagining the
Analytical diagram
Architecture of solitude

Lying awake 2 p.m. to myself
Keep silent
Or tell me different again to whisper
Me to sleep and help invent
Rain against the open window
Circulation space at each level
Continuous Victorian night

Manchester
11 vii 1992

NOVEL

Somewhere after 1848   a village syndic
reins his horse at a ford.
Night sky   half cloud half stars.
Two figures   peasants
cross into the half-light then fade.
Whatever their language
they said nothing.
The appropriation of another's will
is presupposed in the relation of domination.
Then there was a third. The specifications don't matter.
Having no other place to go
in this barely public space
his presence was what he was.
The pathways through narrative
the resistance of Narrative
even in years of plentiful harvest
using discontent to pursue its transforming ends.
What was intended next was far from clear.
The great house was for sale
the keepers' houses empty.
In the shadow of the yard an empty carriage.
And the mirror's depths her body inhabited.
Interior in which no drama unfolded.
The great house   its millions of bricks and stones
the silent unpaid servants
the bent anonymous figures

always in the middle distance
were elsewhere.
Representations   simplifying the world
for pragmatic ends.
At the close of long seigneurial September days.
Sooner or later the riderless horse moves off
uncertainly   keeping out of reach.
Property.
Alone for a night on the plains.
Two peasants reach their thresholds
then sleep.
The parting of the ways
the only convergence here
beyond the fluid obstructions of language
and material structure.
Falling backwards
faster than light the present

Transit Depots

1993

1919

Now they are ringing the bells   Tobacco restrictions have been
removed   Dancing without gloves has become the mode

It is so comprehensible people have become impatient   I have
repeatedly resigned   If you want more time take it

1920

Things are too complicated   A man with one theory is lost
News is surprise   Superstition is easy   The rehearsal will go
on

Who can clear up these misunderstandings

I shall not be able to buy anything here   I wear my son's boots
which are two sizes too large and his castoff suit which is too
narrow in the shoulders

I've now got two endings one comic one tragic

To hell with the page proofs   Thought it was all code   The
songs of the desert might be safer

I'll be sorry for her afterwards

1921

During the election he had not been allowed to say a word

I was startled out of a deep sleep   Not a soul sitting on the
terrasse of the great café   The status of some of these women
is mysterious

I haven't been able to exclude violins altogether

It would always have been thus

1922

The Bank of England acting under the influence of a narrow and obselete doctrine has made a great mistake   Only first-class applicants need apply

For a long time he has no awareness of transition

Support of the treaty means one thing in England another thing in the United States   The clocks are not in unison   Local details exist everywhere

She has made her home in a hotel

Tonight Flaubert's letters

1923

Mr John Hodge made parliamentary history by turning up in a
lemon-coloured shantung suit cream socks and a panama hat
Isolated successes in big cities last two winters

Centralization is inevitable   What's it got to do with you that
people are starving   They divided the country in the way they
thought best

In this city you can't turn round   Everything takes so much
time

Their faces should be immobile and expressionless   An
actress is what you need

1924

Surface has a great future

Motoring up yesterday he had an idea for a revue   The king
obligingly relaxed the rule that Cabinet Ministers should wear
knee-breeches and white silk stockings at royal levees   It's
pleasant that there are so many of them and that they are
interchangeable   The courts are working feverishly

The maitre d'hotel takes no share in the tips   The light
refreshments downstairs weren't free

It seemed impossible to ever find you alone

1925

Permanent abstention means permanent disenfranchisement

Water and atmosphere are transitional regions   Since there
is no canon of vernacular he makes his own

There is nothing I want more than something different

Bones are coordinated to form the skeleton   A stone falls
One bone alone achieves nothing   Increasing in acceleration
it bounces down a steep hill

The eye travels along the paths cut out for it in the work

It is crucial in a fight to be as angry as possible

1926

Doubtless there are patient souls who will wade through anything
for the sake of the possible joke   The daydream of almost every
English boy to drive a train or a bus   He had to find out about
theories of money

The people here are extremely hospitable   Hundreds of people
cleared a way through the crowds of students to the
Konzerthaus   It is almost impossible to tell you about one
night-time scene in the Naples transit depot   The bed and
pillows are softer than the ones I've become used to so I didn't
sleep at all

The story is one of over-equipment and of borrowing to meet
losses with a gradually worsening liquidity

What have you done with the second page of this letter

1927

Securing the freedom of the streets   Wiener Frühstück on
the sunny terrace of the Café Heinrichshof on a July morning
Schlagobers on the coffee   You cannot imagine the physical and
moral degradation to which the ordinary prisoners have
been reduced

At 8.30 am he suspended religious functions to motor into
Metternich's famous Chancellery on the Ballhausplatz

I have a mirror to see myself in   The coffins lay on seventy-five
tall catafalques at the gates of the central cemetery

1928

Fate is no longer an integral power but more like fields of force
to be observed as they send out currents in opposite directions

Every bit as important is the non-printed as well as the printed
surface

We're limited to one request a week and for one thing only

The worst problem I have now is boredom   I arrived in Rome
two days ago

1929

Probably not one motorist in a thousand observes the general
speed limit of twenty miles per hour   Legislation is greatly
overdue

I also have very little desire to write now

There is little to say about this transformation because it is
incomplete

I think of the times I made you cry especially the first time

I have been fighting for years against the instinct to write this
particular novel   No doubt all prison libraries are inconsistent

1930

Why should the rate of interest be so high   I think it is their
intention to wreck South Durham

The venom of Pope is what is needed

In the afternoon on the Leipziger Strasse the windows of
Wertheim Grünfeld and other department stores were smashed
A new beginning a new turn of the wheel   There are walls in
question which are not metaphorical

I wish I could help you   Thankyou for everything you sent me
Two years ago there was no need to be frightened

1931

Any capital spent there would be thrown away   The emergency
has arrived   I have made no change to my will

I live in a series of rooms in different houses   This relativism is
comic and negative

The old ego dies hard

When you get an address send it on   Even with malaria it is
possible to write

1932

Southern Railway Moonlit Walk: Experience the novel thrill of
watching a summer dawn from the first streaks to the full sunrise

Their thoughts are disguised impulses   She refused to be
taken and put leaves over her face   In busy times with their
inability to expand output and having to face increased costs of
scrap they would find it difficult to make profits   Without heroes
they feel nothing   Even here in Italy there's been heavy snow

Take heart I'm not mentioned in any way

1933

In some cases an alteration is specific and definite

I said that to myself under my breath from the beginning

He would like to be something of a popular entertainer   The
theory of monopoly has never been interpreted in this way
They take whatever business comes their way and expect others
to do likewise   This was a possibility that had to be foreseen
You've ceased to be funny   The equilibrium between cost and
price is however only temporary   The passages in red type
should really be in italics   Most patents come to nothing

Later the field of choice is more limited yet rarely is it diminished
to nothing

I apologize for occupying your space

In a few days I will be getting injections of strychnine and
phosphorus

1934

Since the days of the air the old frontiers are gone   One cannot
restore the same monarch twice

At the Vienna Heimwehr headquarters on Herrengasse on
Sunday morning February 18th sandwiches and sherry for the
press   There was no restriction on smoking   I can hardly
remember a thing about Monday

Depth doesn't get you anywhere

In the end I took the manuscript away without saying a word
Minutiae too trifling to print

I shall have nothing to send you   We are all going to vote yes

1935

War and particularly successful war is much more an affair of the
imagination than people think

Treat him as an artifex and all the details fall into place   Hot-
strip steel is a precondition for cold reduction and the latter
cannot substitute for the former   Would it be possible to use
the first lines as titles   The one word which is utterly taboo is
the sacred word 'demarcation'   Take him as anything save the
artist and you'll get muddled in contradictions   In this mood I
would not take on any job at all   I'll be sent proofs I suppose

The Royal School of Needlework designed a Jubilee sampler
that everyone could make decorated with pictures of guns
palaces and yachts

1936

At supper you still see the crumbs from breakfast   For ten
years I've been cut off from the world   The things that oppress
me most are the scraps of newspaper that are scattered all over
the floor   Two men called scuffers shovel the coal onto a
rubber conveyor belt which carries it through a tunnel to the tubs
on the main road where it is hauled by steam-haulage to the
cages

The scene changes to a derelict factory by moonlight

Going into strange houses to hear the wireless announce
another disaster

His suitcases are always packed

1937

It reads like a mystery story to me

Write me a long letter   Above all give pride of place to tempo

1938

Do you think we are really under arrest   As the journey
progressed the tea got nastier tasting increasingly of fish

Markets close firmer   What is shouted from the rooftops is a lie
Cover your tracks   Enter the dream-house   The nearest thing
to hand is Bavarian folk-lore   He had no other means of
livelihood   Something similar may occur in third-rate provincial
theatres   There is room for everything   There were snipe to
eat and rainbow trout

And what were these small children doing standing opposite
each other on either side of the road holding up a little knot of
something with a hopeful gesture

At a given point the word ceases   These intervals are what
matter

1939

To passengers the storm is invisible

At Le Perthus from nine o'clock this morning until 4.30 I have been watching soldiers passing between the two stone posts which are actually the frontier line

Epic theatre and tragic theatre have a very different kind of alliance with the passing of time

I can't answer because they are still there

THREE WEDNESDAYS IN JULY

1998

1

Neighbours' acres

Could anything please her so much?

"Father"

Delivered with proper wistful ennui

A useful accomplishment

Governed by iron internal discipline

Tedium

In Hampshire or somewhere

2

Broken hedge the outer gates

Half hidden

In the parish seek solace

Abandoned faithful

Father's speech she
Speaks from hearsay

To be certain the master
Imagined her good children

3

Lying beside the stove under a blanket she
asked if I'd been born here she
could have been beautiful   sleeping
through the days and the spring the ice
Changing at three o' clock

Each of us supposed to be different

so far away

Love makes the stars move yes
until the last train leaves

There was no hope for us it was
all for you I
Only imagined her

4

Beginning

Inevitable

Another street
Street-corners   wharves

Fictions of space

Surface in the afternoon

And finally the almshouse

From father to child

Her sister's voice

Eyes fixed on the open window darkened
By curtains small
Diamond-shaped panes
Carved globes of wood
Under the jutting storeys

5

Under a white parasol
Pale-faced perfect in shade she spoke

An act of perfect contrition

Tendril following the outline of an arch

East of here the distance never ends

Wind and brightness of the uplands
Cut into hexagons how
Skillfully
Neat clerk's handwriting fenced it in

6

Structures shadowy

Interiors

Murmur of reading

Through the afternoon the familiar

Circle

The wrong house of

Who lived waiting

Books lying everywhere

Wild purpose

Ashes from it all

7

after Baudelaire

i

unaccountable yes
Your
                    glance curving

Space so beautiful   which

Happened
New Oxford Street August
First I

Never knew your name I

Could have loved you you
Knew it too

ii

Where I wish   where she walked
Cuts a line through cause too long
To quote

So beautiful

I never knew her name her hair
Was light
All the bright day scattered

This was true and I went

Away like the morning

About to unhappen

8

    blue shadows
Lapped
Across flowing stonework
The palazzo's facades
Pixel by pixel all
Afternoon ignored us
Trying to remember
What was left of the summer
Cancelled each other out

This year next year sometime never . . .

Glyphs & numerals

9

              tainting the soft

Haze of rain

Neon

Lime and orange

Blurred

Zip of headlights

Alleys and backyards

Secluded rooms

Vacancies

Theories omissions lies

Your wonderful list

Deco lettering in brass

Smudged newsprint

10

       driving South half the night

Or West

Arriving   leaving

For which there's no vernacular I
Listened for a long time

Patch of cloud hurrying the river

White under the moon this empty

Junction the impossible

Present the

PRAGUE /SOFIA

I

action is

word indecipherable

And in the after-vacancy
Black page white letters
What happens to the moment
Something in syntax resists
The air moving
Leaves shining
Surface in
Daylight open or
All that was not there every
Detail

II

Someone's absence you
Dreamed cold into airfields a referent
Perlovska cyrillic moonlit key
Jammed twice in the lock in the dark
Chimney stairs shoulders ache colder
And colder
Rust so everything is
Pointless again the next
Flight

November 1993

LONDON STARTING FROM A : *Forty-Eight Haiku*

A IS FOR

      afterwards it was raining
          outside it was so late
              the streets were empty

      a hundred miles of moonlight
          out there any direction
              the M25

B IS FOR

      bascules of Tower Bridge up
          flawed glass of the Thames
              winter dawn silver

      morning after morning
          dapple of light on grey stone
              water moving

C IS FOR

      Ratcliffe low red cliff
          lifted out of the marsh curved
              south then receded

      strokes of distant hammers
          tinkle of a bell fluttering
              birds & silence

D IS FOR

      sounds the ducks make sleeping
          as if they had something
              to say in their dreams

E IS FOR

        double row of elms
            wide grassy avenues bright
                window of bare sky

      a five-arched stone bridge
            the solemn gloom of E-flat
                the Long Water

F IS FOR

        bone hill fields Sunday
            the faintest breeze carries the
                sound of the bronze bell

G IS FOR

        Plate one 1946
            St Paul's Cathedral
                through the willow-herb

        how many City churches
            rise above structures now
                surrounding them

        St Antholin's spire
            Watling Street still in a
                Sydenham back garden

H IS FOR

        scratchy leaves thick on the paths
            Holland Park a whole
                city ochre & grey

I IS FOR

      an apparition
          sound of pages being turned
             grey fabric of dawn

      the resistance of things
          shadows of bridge & gate
             voices etched in stone

J is for

      trams in South London
          their stronghold held out until
          1952

K is for

      sky a pale coast
          low black smoking rainclouds
             endless Holborn afternoons

L IS FOR

      not wind enough to
          twirl the one red leaf the sky
             amazingly blank

      bright pavilions
          of shadow she let the red
             leaf float out to him

M IS FOR

      Bond Street Saturday
          mahogany chinese silk
             & magnolia

N is for

  archives of the city
   carted away from Guildhall
    & burned unread

  wilderness of angled tiles
   rinsed in soft rain silver
    light enchanted

O is for

  sound of feet tramping
   on fallen leaves thick against
    every damp surface

  moon rising before
   dark the chestnut trees' patterns
    gathering twilight

P is for

  bare trees interlacing each
   other's black branches
    winter arrangements

  towers pale shadows
   loom in misty rain discoloured
    copper gaslight flares

Q is for

  information in
   Selfridge's windows the sky
    higher than usual

R is for

> Battersea Buddha
>> Friday morning's fifteen ways
>>> of describing rain

S is for

> unsure horizons Shadwell
>> Basin a mass of ships
>>> their crowded masts

> slate-grey plain of water
>> northern bank's hazy
>>> horizon sleeping clouds

> sombre hulls brown sails
>> balancing a white seabird
>>> chill water shimmers

> rainy april evening
>> surrey river skyline
>>> scribbled on shadows

T is for

> sixteen eighty-three
>> crossing the Thames dryshod
>>> footprints in soft grey ash

> from Temple to Southwark
>> sledges horses and carts
>>> plied their trade on ice

U is for

    useless to explain
        if the real is what happens
            damp leaves smouldering

    motionless blue cirrus
        clouds of tobacco smoke one
            flickering lamp

V is for

    the Eastern hotel
        nights where two roads meet at the
            cold rim of the world

    surface suddenly caught
        in a monochrome flash now
            in moonlight gone

W IS FOR

    "since last year we parted"
        empty boat tipped
            in the soft mud at low tide

    rhomboid sails bronze and gold
        apparitions
            at the edge of sunset

    Wapping Old Stairs
        no masts now a stranger's knowledge
            bird-tracks on grey silt

    bright wedge of daylight
        between black walls a steamer
            outward bound then gone

X is for
>south to the river
>>between Blackfriars and
>>>London Bridge wandering

>the sharp wind in a
>>thousand alleys fifty ways
>>>of describing cold

Y is for
>cloudy clear windy
>>rainy & bright this april
>>>august afternoon

Z is for
>half moon through a
>>ring of mist over the western
>>>face of somewhere else

>light snow powders slates
>>temperatures of moonlight
>>>somebody else's dream

DIVIDED INTO ONE

2004

I

As night
falls in a long November coda
kiln-fires lurid
smears on the fog and the last
light drains out
across the desolate flats below Tilbury
where riverside dykes bright grass
confine London's seething
rubbish and the northern foreshore vertically
below Trinity High Water the receding
tide revealed circular daub-and-wattle sheds
a great spread of Roman pottery stretched for two hundred
yards in an icy drawer
beneath a fluctuating canopy of tide
and tidal mud   descending
scales against a tinkling purl-man's bell
clicking of the capstan palls
zephyr and the plash of Thames
merge and dissolve
distance   salt air
shadows

II

The Queen was
brought
by water to
Whitehall

At every stroke the
oars did
tears
fall

III

What's it called
Steam of surfaces you dream of
The ragged tear in the fabric
Crack in the spire
What is it
They imagine hurrying where
Units of what presence in
Ghostly halflight repeated
Out of yesterday the new
Silence at the core of this noise art
Changes appearance into appearance
In new shapes unexpected
Statuary of whose hand of
What substance hurrying this way
Targeted from a great distance
Nettles and lichen waiting
If it coheres or if it doesn't
End-stopped   rendezvous

IV

In the midst of danger distance
Thinking ourselves
What the language tells us
Isn't there   out of danger
A kind of half whisper
Breathing death in every place the
Face of London
Mask of a mask through a linen sheet
The dead-cart's night errand
Spreading from that house to
Other houses
By the visible unwary conversing
Strangers dangerous
Rich and poor together
And people have it that know it not
And none knows how far to carry that back
Or where to stop
For none knows when or where or how or
From whom
The others their neighbours
Burning brimstone pitch gunpowder
Keeping within doors
Both sides of the wall
In absolute loneliness
A million of people in a body together

V

Blackfriars

Live brands
Lodged by the wind

A shower of fire-drops

Blood-red disc
Dim through the smoke
Dreamed through the dark

All in one flame's thunder
As far as the Steelyard the East wind
High and driving it
From one burning house to the next
Into the City's heart

Mantle of soot and
Charred fragments

Melted lead

Molten bell metal

Burning pepper

Gog and Magog
No part of it
Burned with the rest

VI

Walking in the Streets of
London in an Alley Musick
in the Market-place Coffee
in every street the ruin
of this island in every Man
the Power of Art to
produce is the true orthodox
Tread upon Fairy Ground the
spells of pickpockets enchantments
of Intoxication in a Tavern
Love Beauty the Incantations of
Pleasure in one place
Poore mens paines and labours

VII

Piers of Southwark Bridge honeycombed
Floating logs of timber lashed together
And every stationary boat and barge
Arrowheads splitting the current

Coronets of lamps
                light the black stream
     beneath
           down to the ocean

                    and soon yon brilliant towers
rooftops steeples chimneys
streets and parks
islands looming out of a hazy sea
cloud-towers by ghostly masons wrought
shall darken with the wave of her wand darken
and shrink and shiver into black specks amid a waste of
dreary sand low-built mudwalled barbarian settlements how
changed from this fair city

VIII

A break between housetops
And the moon's white cities and opal lakes silver heights cloudless

Starless urban night the stars
Pivot   rising and setting

East & West & North & South

At the far horizon's rim
Each within the other invisible towards the four points

IX

Minute particulars everything exists and
not one sigh nor smile
nor tear one hair nor
particle of dust not one

can pass away they
stand at their doors in shadowy
thoroughfares where the city ends
the sky begins and watch

the marvellous West asleep in
endless light it was all
golden and shining when we
came out of the lamplit

church and the organ was
booming and the sky was
very bright and warm and red
but in the gardens

by degrees the twilight came
and the lights faded out
of the sky and the river
Temple Church Evensong 1861

X

St Pancras

Listen to the rain
Through cracks and crevices and broken
Panes the day begins in
Disappointment   dream us
Different again the crowded syllables
Through the poorhouse door things
Profitable must continue
The spatial order the social
Squalor of
Somers Town Agar Town
Built on broken bottles and oyster shells
A few wet sole-skins drying on a line
The landlord the bailiff and the police in
Different voices
Ordinary as brick
Fluttering green rag of a window blind the
Organization of unhappiness
Because because
Behind the gothic violence of St Pancras
Sky blazing into defeat
West
Parapet and projection
Angles and boundaries
Incisions of the chisel
Copper surfaces
Liquids it's impossible to decipher
The exact time it feels like
Autumn

Loose masonry crashing to the ground

XI

laws of light and
air corrosive properties of
atmosphere
glazed white bricks
in subways under railway
arches to deflect and
concentrate light ricochets off
the wall protesting against
shadows dim wet
pavement's shimmering streaks of
gaslight and drizzle Limehouse
St George's
Ratcliffe Shadwell

XII

Herne Hill

A slender rivulet
here trickled there loitered
in long grass clear pools

veils of duckweed
fresh-water shells
skipping shrimps and tadpoles

in their time the summer shadows
purple thistles in autumn
blackberry hedges

in spring primrose
white archangel daisies
first buds the hawthorn

along Croxsted Lane

now by the Half-moon
at the bottom of Herne Hill
a deep-rutted grassless
heavy-hillocked cart-road

diverging gateless into
various brickfields or waste
bordered on each side by
fields dug up for building

or cut through into
gaunt corners
by the wild crossings
of three railroads
and nooks of blind ground

heaps of mixed of
every unclean thing that can
crumble in drought
and mildew that can rot or rust in damp

ashes and rags
beer-bottles
old shoes battered pans smashed crockery
shreds of nameless clothes
iron rotten timber jagged with out-torn nails
cigar-ends
pipe-bowls
cinders
bones and ordure

and variously kneaded into
sticking to
fluttering over all
these remnants broadcast
of newspaper advertisement or big-lettered bill
festering and flaunting out their last publicity in the pits
                              of stinking dust and . . .

after Ruskin 1880

XIII

Inside the gallery looking West
spaces by Veronese
porticoes of radiance in which
governments rose and fell

humour his whim he
deserves the world to himself
a single figure
mounting the staircase the great

barrel-vaulted hall a colourless
dust across opaque surfaces
alabaster pedestals of
red porphyry white

waistcoats the footmen in groups
chamberlains in livery and
talk is only a murmur
of violins in the vast

expanse of
palaces of Ind at every
turn the pick of a dozen
civilizations   the walls

close enough to touch
red and gold embossed
leather screen deflect

avert obstruct

erase

sound-waves of a
troubled world   washed
streets in blue

dawn blurred quarter
moon raw

fogs of a London marsh

XIV

DAN CULLEN, DOCKER
London 1903

a low-ceilinged hole seven feet by eight
his home one of the Municipal Dwellings
not far from Leman Street

bare floor walls covered with blood
marks of squashed insects
and cheap pictures of Garibaldi Engels

John Burns in his blue reefer suit
and white straw hat
and other labour leaders he knew

his Shakespeare and read
history sociology economics
in the watches of the night

and spoke his mind freely
chosen leader of the fruit porters
fires of the spirit

and after the Great Dock Strike
1889 and every day for years
marked and resolutely disciplined

drilled and starved
and soul harrowed and
broken hearted

feet swollen with dropsy he
sat up on the side of the bed
all day a thin blanket

on his legs an old coat
around his shoulders
penniless demanding his discharge

from Whitechapel Infirmary
though they told him he'd die
on the stairs

alone and finally
gasping for breath
baffled on a pauper's couch

in a charity ward
out of the way   the poor
of the earth

hide themselves lonely
together ungrateful
remembered

XV

Measureless instant over the black North Sea

Little or no ventilation or space

Sea-sick too and laid up

A quadrant an almanac an epitome

XVI

Isle of Dogs

The ruin of capital o the perfect
Indicators liquid spirals at the
Dock's edge decorative
Cranes high colonnades white stone
Throwing off snow or rain the
Roof mask's orbed surfaces
Cornice of the pediment
Contours and radius
Index futures burning into the
Air thick with ghosts you
Laboured and failed
Forgot your names
Froze at the railings on a straw sack
Whatever you wanted
In line at the spike winding
Corridors in the dark and the crooked
Turn of the stair this is
Not anybody's home
This is not anybody's speech   nameless
Blind labourer earned his living
Reading aloud in the street feeling
With his fingers the raised letters
But could do nothing now
"The touch was cold"
The birds he said
In spirals over the river
Must be cold   my son four
Shivering against the wall
So far away

Was what I remember here as
Is what I remembered
Divided into one

XVII

Sparkling frosty
moonlit mornings
or

lavender evenings
a million hours ago
parlours

in pier-glass doubled
golden through muslin
Empire

outlined in light a
million specks dancing
bright patch of carpet

clawed foot table
horse-hair chair
lifted to

sit where here was
like morning
for the

child in love with
maps the nations
at sunset heartbroken

Lightning Source UK Ltd.
Milton Keynes UK
UKOW042109271112

202880UK00001B/255/A

9 780907 562634